A TRUE BOOK

REDISCOVERING THE TITANIC

Michael Burgan

Children's Press®
An imprint of Scholastic Inc.

Content Consultant
Tim Maltin, *Titanic* author and historian

Library of Congress Cataloging-in-Publication Data
Names: Burgan, Michael, author.
Title: Rediscovering the Titanic/by Michael Burgan.
Other titles: True book.
Description: First edition. | New York: Children's Press, an imprint of Scholastic, Inc., 2022. | Series: A true book | Includes bibliographical references and index. | Audience: Ages 8–10 | Audience: Grades 4–6 | Summary: "Next set in A TRUE BOOK series. Young readers rediscover the story of the largest and most luxurious ship ever built, The Titanic. Featuring historical imagery, first-hand accounts, and lively text"— Provided by publisher.
Identifiers: LCCN 2022002392 (print) | LCCN 2022002393 (ebook) | ISBN 9781338840568 (library binding) | ISBN 9781338840575 (paperback) | ISBN 9781338840582 (ebk)
Subjects: LCSH: Ballard, Robert D.—Juvenile literature. | Titanic (Steamship)—Juvenile literature. | Shipwrecks—North Atlantic Ocean—Juvenile literature. | Underwater exploration—North Atlantic Ocean—Juvenile literature.
Classification: LCC G530.T6 B849 2022 (print) | LCC G530.T6 (ebook) | DDC 910/.91634—dc23/eng/20220221
LC record available at https://lccn.loc.gov/2022002392
LC ebook record available at https://lccn.loc.gov/2022002393

10 9 8 7 6 5 4 3 2 1   23 24 25 26 27

Printed in China 62
First edition, 2023

Design by Kathleen Petelinsek
Series produced by Spooky Cheetah Press

Front cover: A still from the movie *Raise the Titanic*; (top) a section of the hull; (bottom) the RMS Titanic Inc. expedition of 1996

Back cover: Robert Ballard with *Jason Jr.*

Find the Truth!

Everything you are about to read is true *except* for one of the sentences on this page.

Which one is **TRUE**?

T or F The *Titanic* was first found by a small underwater craft called *Alvin*.

T or F The wreck of the *Titanic* is now a reef—home to fish, crabs, and corals.

Find the answers in this book.

What's in This Book?

The Titanic found

Luxury liner sank in 1912, killing 1,513

St. John's, Newfoundland (UPI)—Scientists yesterday found the wreckage of the Titanic, the "unsinkable" luxury liner that struck an iceberg on its maiden voyage and sank in 1912, the leader of a joint U.S.-French expedition said.

Dr. Robert Ballard of the Woods Hole Oceanographic Institution in Massachusetts said in a ship-to-shore interview that pieces of the ship were located at 13,000 feet shortly after midnight Sunday about 370 miles south of Newfoundland.

"To finally put those souls to rest was a very nice feeling," said Ballard. "We came on it early this morning. It was just bang, there it was right on top of it."

Ballard headed the U.S. expedition on board

huge area and we decided to pull up and get above it all."

THE TITANIC, which its builder called unsinkable, sank on its maiden voyage with the loss of 1,513 lives on April 15, 1912. The pride of Britain's White Star Line was the biggest and most luxurious liner of its era.

Ballard said the search team's initial reaction "was excitement, then a coming down off that to realize that we had found the ship where ... people had died. (For) a

A newspaper announces Robert Ballard's discovery of the *Titanic*.

These dishes were found at the *Titanic* wreck site.

The **BIG** Truth

A *Titanic* Debate

This is one of the *Titanic*'s huge boilers.

Searching for the *Titanic*

Most people have heard of the ship called the *Titanic* and the tragic tale of its sinking on the night of **April 14–15, 1912,** after hitting an iceberg. The story is famous around the world. But history is filled with shipwrecks, including some that had a much greater loss of life. So why are people still **fascinated by the *Titanic*,** more than **100 years after** it sank?

The *Titanic* **was world-famous** long before it set sail. After all, the *Titanic* and its twin ship, the *Olympic*, were the **largest ships ever built** at the time. And the most **luxurious.**

Many people **believed the *Titanic* could not sink.** But it did—on its very first voyage. Ever since that fateful night, the *Titanic*'s story has continued to grow in people's imagination. This is the story of how—and why—Robert Ballard went **searching for the wreck of the *Titanic* at the bottom of the ocean.** And how he and his crew found it after it had been underwater for more than 70 years.

An illustration of the *Titanic* sailing across the Atlantic.

The *Titanic*'s route

Southampton, England

New York City

U.S.

ATLANTIC OCEAN

Where the *Titanic* sank

This ill
shows
steami
North A

A Difficult Hunt

Almost from the time it sank, people had thought about looking for the *Titanic*. Some wanted to raise the wreck. Some wanted to film it. Others hoped to remove items from the ship. But no one knew the exact spot where the famous ship sank. Hundreds of people had survived after the ship crashed into the iceberg. From their lifeboats, these survivors saw the ship go down. So how is it that no one knew the exact spot where a huge ship like the *Titanic* had sunk? Several things made it hard to hunt for the shipwreck.

Nature at Work

Ocean **currents** presented one challenge to finding the *Titanic*'s remains. A current is horizontal movement in ocean water. The ocean currents are strong in the part of the Atlantic Ocean where the *Titanic* sank. The currents moved the ship while it was still on the surface— and as it sank. The currents also moved the lifeboats. By the time the rescue ship, the *Carpathia*, arrived to pick up the survivors, the lifeboats had drifted away from the wreck.

A Navigation Error

Another problem resulted from a mistake made on the night the *Titanic* sank. Before sending out a distress signal, Fourth Officer Joseph Boxhall had to determine the ship's exact location. He started with the position taken by Second Officer Charles Lightoller at 7:30 that night. Then Boxhall estimated how far the ship had traveled since then, and the direction it took. But the position recorded by Lightoller was wrong. So that made Boxhall's wrong, too. The position the *Titanic* broadcast in its distress message was about 10 miles away from where the ship really was.

A radio operator on a nearby ship received the *Titanic*'s distress message and wrote it down. It gives the *Titanic*'s position as latitude N 41°46', longitude W 50°14'.

A Deep Plunge

Even if explorers had known exactly where to look for the *Titanic*, they faced another major problem. The ship sank in waters about 12,500 feet (3,810 meters) deep. Submarines in 1912 could not reach those depths—and they would not be able to for decades. It would take more than 60 years after the sinking for engineers to develop the technology that could both reach that depth and easily search for the *Titanic*.

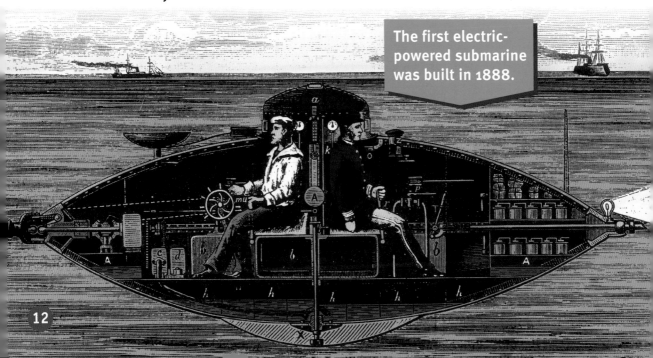

The first electric-powered submarine was built in 1888.

Grimm's team and the sonar equipment they used (right)

Early Efforts

In 1980, Jack Grimm used some of that new technology, including **sonar,** to search for the *Titanic*. Sonar uses sound waves to locate objects underwater. The Deep Two sonar is designed to be towed by a ship on the surface. Grimm's crew used it on the first trip to explore the area and then added special underwater video cameras on two later trips, but they could not find the wreck. Meanwhile, explorer Robert Ballard closely followed Grimm's searches. He was also really interested in the wreck of the *Titanic*.

13

Robert Ballard saw *20,000 Leagues Under the Sea* when he was 12 years old. The movie inspired his dream to explore the oceans.

Ballard with an underwater craft he used to explore the *Titanic*

Finding the *Titanic* at Last

Robert Ballard grew up in San Diego, California, a city on the coast of the Pacific Ocean. When he was still a kid, he learned to scuba dive so he could make his first ocean explorations. In college, Ballard studied **marine geology** and then became an oceanographer. An oceanographer is a scientist who studies oceans and the creatures in them. Ballard's fascination with the sea would ultimately lead him on his hunt for the *Titanic*.

The Woods Hole Oceanographic Institute is in Massachusetts.

A Navy Scientist

While Ballard was studying oceanography, he joined the navy. In 1967, he was assigned to the Woods Hole Oceanographic Institute. He worked with the institute's scientists who studied the deepest parts of the ocean and often did research for the navy. In their work, the scientists sometimes used a small underwater vehicle called a **submersible**. After Ballard left active duty with the navy and finished his studies, he began working at Woods Hole. He often made deep ocean dives in a submersible.

A Failed Mission

While Ballard was at Woods Hole, he had gotten a chance to look for the *Titanic* even before Jack Grimm. In 1977, he had used a ship called the *Seaprobe* that could drop 3,000 feet (914 m) of pipes deep into the ocean. A pod at the end of the last pipe held sonar equipment as well as video and still cameras. But when the structure was extended as far as it could go, it broke. The entire rigging and all the equipment sank to the bottom of the ocean. The mission was a failure.

Because of the accident on the *Seaprobe*, Ballard lost equipment worth $600,000.

The *Seaprobe* was specially designed for deep-sea research.

Introducing *Argo*

Almost 10 years later, Ballard got another chance to look for the *Titanic*—and a better tool for the **expedition**. Ballard had helped the navy design an imaging sled called *Argo* that was towed by a cable connecting it to a surface ship. *Argo* carried sonar and three video cameras that could send live images to the ship. And it could explore the ocean at depths of more than 12,000 feet (3,658 m). In 1985, Ballard announced that he was using *Argo* to look for the *Titanic*. But that was just part of the story.

The USS *Scorpion* is one of the subs Ballard was sent to examine.

A Secret Mission

During the 1960s, two American submarines had sunk in the Atlantic Ocean. They were powered by nuclear engines. If damaged, those engines could release a deadly form of energy called radiation. In 1984, the navy had given Ballard a top secret mission: use *Argo* to see if any radiation had leaked from the subs. Ballard explored the first sub. Then, in 1985, he was given three weeks to use *Argo*. Navy officials said he could hunt for the *Titanic*—but only after he examined the second submarine. Ballard had to work fast if he wanted to have time to look for the *Titanic*! And he did. Neither sub's engine had leaked radiation.

In the Zone

On August 24, 1985, Ballard and his crew reached the area where the *Titanic* sank. They had only nine days left to use *Argo* to hunt for the shipwreck. Their ship, the *Knorr,* was not carrying only *Argo.* It was carrying another towed imaging sled called *ANGUS.* Photos from *ANGUS* were not uploaded right to the ship. The film from the camera had to be developed, but the photos were more detailed than those from *Argo.*

Ballard posing next to *ANGUS* during the expedition

Ballard aboard the *Knorr* (left) and the exterior of the ship (right)

Looking for Clues

Ballard was unsure of where to look. He hoped his advanced equipment would help him find a **debris** field from the shipwreck. One witness of the sinking thought the ship broke in two. If it had, many items would have spilled out and settled on the ocean floor—creating a debris field. Ballard believed that if he found the debris field, it would lead him to the wreck.

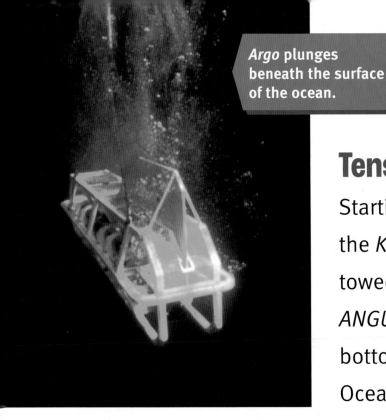

Argo plunges beneath the surface of the ocean.

Tense Times

Starting on August 25, the *Knorr* slowly towed *Argo* and *ANGUS* over the bottom of the Atlantic Ocean. But their cameras could not find a trace of the *Titanic*. The operation was repeated over the next two days with no success. On August 28, *Argo* explored near where the *Carpathia* had rescued passengers in the lifeboats. Then the robot had its own accident. A problem with the cable connecting *Argo* to the ship forced the crew to let *Argo* crash onto the ocean bottom. Luckily, the crew was able to rescue *Argo*, and the search continued.

Success!

Ballard was running out of time to use *Argo*. Then, shortly after midnight on September 1, 1985, he was called to the control room. The crew showed him what *Argo*'s cameras had just detected—a large, round metal object. It was a boiler for the kind of steam engine that had powered the *Titanic*. Finally, the *Knorr* crew had found the famous wreck!

The Titanic found

Luxury liner sank in 1912, killing 1,513

St. John's, Newfoundland (UPI)—Scientists yesterday found the wreckage of the Titanic, the "unsinkable" luxury liner that struck an iceberg on its maiden voyage and sank in 1912, the leader of a

The *Knorr* research crew and a newspaper story about their discovery

In 1977, Robert Ballard was part of a team of scientists that used *Alvin* to find sea creatures no one had seen before.

An illustration of the *Titanic*'s bow at the bottom of the ocean

Treasures on the Ocean Bottom

Along with spotting the boiler and other debris, Robert Ballard saw that the **hull** of the ship had indeed broken into two major pieces. They sat about 2,000 feet (609 m) apart. News quickly spread that Ballard had found the *Titanic*. His discovery excited people around the world. In July 1986, Ballard and his crew returned to the spot where they had found the wreck. This time, Ballard brought *Alvin*, a deep-sea submersible that could carry people.

The wreck of the Titanic is now a reef. It is home to several species of fish, crabs, and corals.

This is what it looks like inside *Alvin*'s crew pod.

Up Close to *Titanic*

For this expedition, Ballard and his crew sailed on a ship called *Atlantis II*. On July 13, 1986, Ballard set out for the deep in *Alvin*. With him were Ralph Hollis, the submersible's pilot, and copilot Dudley Foster. The trip to the ocean bottom took more than two hours. Hollis then followed directions sent from the crew on *Atlantis II*. Soon Ballard spotted part of the *Titanic*'s **bow**. He slowly let out his breath as he saw the ship with his own eyes. Ballard and the other two divers were the first people to get close to the wreck of the *Titanic*.

A Deep Diver

Scientists at Woods Hole designed *Alvin* to explore depths of 13,000 feet (3,962 m). The submersible's equipment included sonar, a video camera, and still cameras. *Alvin* also held three people. The space was so tight, they often had to sit cross-legged on the floor. As *Alvin* plunged deeper into the ocean, the water outside it grew colder. Its passengers had to put on extra sweaters to stay warm. The pressure of the water against *Alvin* increased as it dove down. Its strong metal hull kept the divers inside safe from the crushing force.

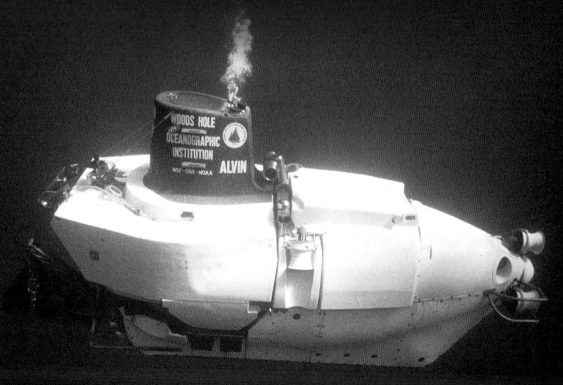

Turn to pages 42 and 43 for a detailed illustration of Alvin.

Jason Jr. "looks" into one of the Titanic's staterooms.

In 1991, Jason Jr. was lost at sea in an accident.

The Newest Tool

Ballard had *Argo* and *ANGUS* for this expedition, as well as a new robot called *Jason Jr*. The crew called it "*JJ*" for short. *JJ* was on its first mission in deep waters. It was smaller than *Argo* and could go farther into the wreckage. *JJ* was connected to *Alvin* by a long cable that was 300 feet (91 m) long, and the crew on *Alvin* controlled its movements. *JJ* carried both a still camera and a video camera and sent its images back to *Alvin*.

Ready to Explore

Once *Alvin* reached the ocean bottom, the crew had about three hours to explore the wreck. Ballard could see that the *Titanic* had turned into an artificial reef where fish were living. He also saw long pieces of rust hanging down from the ship. The rust formed as **bacteria** ate away at the steel. Ballard named what he saw "rusticles." For more than a week, Ballard made several more dives to the wreckage.

Robert Ballard's new word, *rusticle*, is now found in some dictionaries.

A rusticle on the *Titanic*

A Closer Look

On one dive, *JJ* entered the *Titanic* and spotted the ship's grand staircase. *JJ*, *ANGUS*, and *Alvin* also explored the debris field. Their cameras saw several **artifacts**, including three safes, dishes and a copper sink from the kitchen, a toilet bowl, and a glass bottle that had not broken. Among *ANGUS*'s photos was one of a pair of shoes that someone on the *Titanic* had worn.

The bronze part of this deck bench remains, but the wooden seat has rotted away.

A Question Answered?

For years, many people wondered how the *Titanic* could sink so quickly. Most assumed the iceberg created a long gash in its hull. But Ballard did not see evidence of that. He saw several bent steel plates and found that the steel bolts holding them in place had popped out. The crash with the iceberg probably caused this damage in several spots, creating small openings that let in water. In 1998, research on the bolts seemed to prove this theory. They were not designed to withstand the enormous force of the collision.

A *Titanic* Debate

By law, because Robert Ballard discovered the wreck in 1985, he could have owned everything he found—if he had taken it to the surface. But he didn't want to disturb the site. However, other explorers who visited the wreck after him did remove items and brought them to the surface. Some still hope to remove more items from the site. What do you think is the right thing to do? Take more artifacts or leave the wreck alone? Read on to learn arguments supporting both positions!

Take More Artifacts

- Artifacts taken from the wreck are sometimes displayed. Thanks to that, everybody can learn more about the *Titanic* and its sinking.
- Artifacts that are put on display serve as a memorial, or a way to remember what happened to the *Titanic* and all the people who died in the tragedy.
- Items from the ship—and the ship itself—that remain in the ocean are being destroyed by salt water and sea creatures. Removing those pieces of history assures that they are not lost forever.

These binoculars from the *Titanic* are on display.

The *Titanic*'s breakfast dishes have been left undisturbed underwater.

Leave the Wreck Alone

- The wreck is like a cemetery. The place where so many people died should not be disturbed. Several relatives of the survivors from the *Titanic* agree.
- On some missions to retrieve artifacts, submersibles have damaged parts of the wreck. For example, part of the **crow's nest** was destroyed and some of the deck was dented.
- Instead of taking artifacts and parts of the ship, they can be filmed. The images taken can be shared with the world.

In 2001, an American couple got married in a submersible while it sat on the *Titanic*.

The *Nautile* is a deep-sea submersible that has been used to explore the *Titanic*.

IFREMER

NAUTILE

More Explorations

In 1987, a French expedition visited the site of the shipwreck. The trip was made in partnership with an American company that would later name itself RMS Titanic Inc. The team brought along a submersible called *Nautile*, which—like *Alvin*—is able to carry three researchers. The expedition was considered a "salvage" trip, meaning the purpose was to bring artifacts from the *Titanic* up to the surface.

History from the Deep

Between 1987 and 2004, RMS Titanic Inc. made seven trips to the wreck site. The company brought up a total of about 6,000 artifacts. Those include a gold bracelet with the name "Amy" spelled out in diamonds. A $10 bill was found inside a leather wallet. And a man's hat, called a bowler, was found in relatively good shape, despite being underwater for decades.

Timeline: The Hunt for the *Titanic*

1977
Robert Ballard's first mission to find the *Titanic*, aboard the *Seaprobe*, ends in failure.

1980
Jack Grimm makes the first of three expeditions to find the *Titanic* but can't locate it.

1985
Near the end of a secret mission for the navy, Ballard and his crew find the *Titanic*.

1986
Inside the *Alvin* submersible, Ballard sees parts of the wreck up close for the first time.

RMS Titanic Inc. also found a bronze statue of a small angel. It most likely stood on the ship's main staircase. Other items include eyeglasses, dishes, luggage, and pieces of coal that powered the ship's giant engines. The smallest items found were clay marbles that most likely belonged to one of the children on the *Titanic*. In 1998, the company brought the largest artifact to the surface—a piece of the hull that weighed 20 tons.

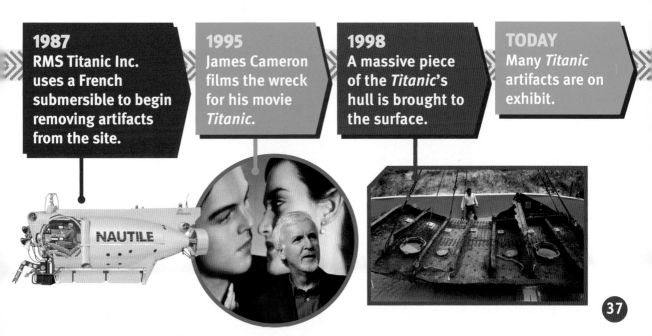

1987
RMS Titanic Inc. uses a French submersible to begin removing artifacts from the site.

1995
James Cameron films the wreck for his movie *Titanic*.

1998
A massive piece of the *Titanic*'s hull is brought to the surface.

TODAY
Many *Titanic* artifacts are on exhibit.

NAUTILE

See for Yourself

Most of us will never have a chance to dive down 12,500 feet (3,810 m) in a submersible and explore the *Titanic*. But several exhibits around the world offer a glimpse of what was found at the wreck. There are four such exhibits in the United States alone! Items on display include luggage, the ship's giant bronze whistles, and a full bottle of champagne. You can also see a pocket watch and one of the ship's deck chairs.

This *Titanic* museum is in Pigeon Forge, Tennessee.

Today, tourists can pay $250,000 to visit the Titanic.

A perfectly preserved cup sits among the debris.

The Future of the *Titanic*

In 2020, the United States and the United Kingdom signed a treaty to protect the *Titanic* artifacts that are still in the ocean. This law has already stopped some salvaging expeditions. People can still explore the wreck. But less of the *Titanic* remains—and it continues to disappear. Thanks in part to Robert Ballard's expeditions, the legendary *Titanic* will never be forgotten.

Clues from the Past

We learn about the past through primary sources. These include objects or written materials that were created at the time of the event being studied. When Ballard and his crew were getting ready for the expedition to search for the *Titanic*, they used materials that would help them recognize parts of the ship when they saw them. Here are just two of the primary sources they used.

This is the boiler that let Ballard know he had found the *Titanic*. Each of the boilers was as tall as a three-story house.

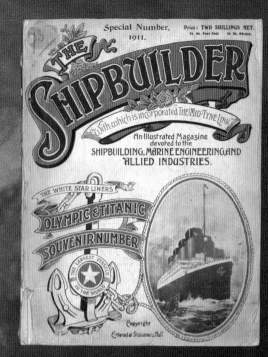

Shipbuilder Magazine

An article published in 1911 in *Shipbuilder* magazine explained how the *Titanic* and its twin ship, the *Olympic*, had been built. Ballard and his crew used the article to learn about the ship.

Photograph

The article in *Shipbuilder* magazine included this original photo of the boilers—the big machines that powered the ship by burning coal. There were 24 of them on the *Titanic*. When the crew spotted one of the original boilers on the ocean floor, they compared it with the one in the photograph to confirm that they had found the *Titanic*!

DEEPER DIVE

DEEPER DIVE

PARTS OF
Alvin

Thrusters

Alvin has seven thrusters. Three move the submersible backward and forward. Two move *Alvin* up and down, and two help it turn.

Titanium Frame

Alvin's titanium frame protects the researchers inside from the crushing pressure of the deep sea.

Ballast Tanks

Some of these tanks hold water, which can be released or taken in to help *Alvin* sink or rise.

Batteries

The batteries power *Alvin* and its electronics. They need to be recharged after every use.

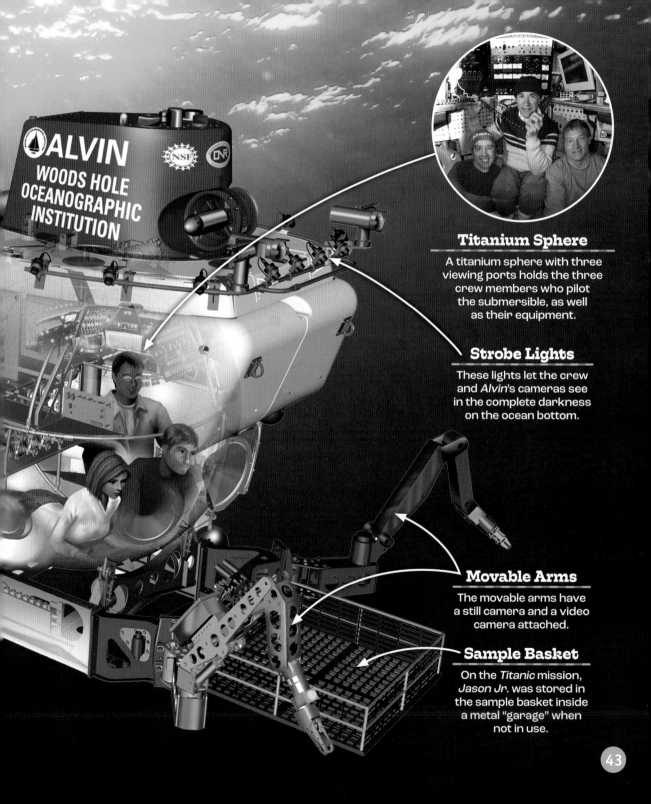

Titanium Sphere

A titanium sphere with three viewing ports holds the three crew members who pilot the submersible, as well as their equipment.

Strobe Lights

These lights let the crew and *Alvin*'s cameras see in the complete darkness on the ocean bottom.

Movable Arms

The movable arms have a still camera and a video camera attached.

Sample Basket

On the *Titanic* mission, *Jason Jr.* was stored in the sample basket inside a metal "garage" when not in use.

ALVIN
WOODS HOLE
OCEANOGRAPHIC
INSTITUTION

NSF   ONR

True Statistics

Number of shipwrecks thought to be in the oceans today: more than three million

Location of the wreck of the *Titanic*: about 380 miles (612 km) southeast of Newfoundland, Canada

Distance between the two main pieces of the *Titanic* on the ocean bottom: about 2,000 feet (609 m)

Number of expeditions Robert Ballard has made to explore the world's oceans: more than 150

Number of dives Robert Ballard and his crew made in *Alvin* on the 1986 expedition: 12

Total number of dives *Alvin* has made, as of 2021: more than 5,000

Cost to buy a piece of coal taken from the *Titanic*: just under $30

Did you find the truth?

(F) The *Titanic* was first found by a small underwater craft called *Alvin*.

(T) The wreck of the *Titanic* is now a reef—home to fish, crabs, and corals.

Resources

Other books in this series:

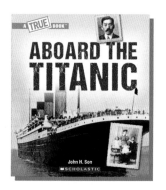 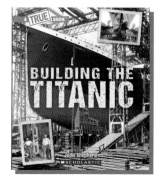 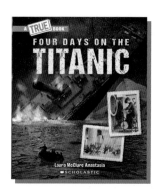

You can also look at:

Benoit, Peter. *The Titanic*. New York: Scholastic, 2013.

Burgan, Michael. *Finding the Titanic: How Images from the Ocean Depths Fueled Interest in the Doomed Ship*. North Mankato, MN: Compass Point Books, 2018.

Smith, Miranda. *Titanic*. London: Scholastic, 2014.

Yount, Lisa. *Robert Ballard: Explorer and Undersea Archaeologist*. New York: Chelsea House, 2009.

Glossary

artifacts (AHR-tuh-fakts) objects made or changed by human beings, especially a tool or weapon used in the past

bacteria (bak-TEER-ee-uh) tiny, single-celled living things that exist everywhere and that can either be useful or harmful

bow (bou) the front section of a ship or boat

crow's nest (KROHZ nest) a small platform used for a lookout found on a sailing ship's mast

currents (KUR-uhnts) the movement of water in a definite direction in a river or an ocean

debris (duh-BREE) the pieces of something that has been broken or destroyed

expedition (ek-spuh-DISH-uhn) a long trip made for a specific purpose, such as for exploration

hull (huhl) the frame or body of a boat or ship

marine geology (muh-REEN jee-AH-luh-jee) the study of the physical structure of the ocean

sonar (SOH-nahr) an instrument used on ships and submarines that sends out underwater sound waves to determine the location of objects and the distance to the bottom

submersible (suhb-MUR-suh-buhl) a small underwater craft used for deep-sea research

Index

Page numbers in **bold** indicate illustrations.

About the Author

For more than 25 years, Michael Burgan has written more than 300 books for children and teens. His favorite subjects are US history and biographies of famous people. To write this book on the discovery of the wreck of the *Titanic*, he relied mostly on the writings of Robert Ballard. Also helpful was information from the Woods Hole Oceanographic Institute's website. Michael became interested in big passenger ships like the *Titanic* after sailing on several when he was a child. One of them was longer than the *Titanic*! Michael studied history at the University of Connecticut. He currently lives in Santa Fe, New Mexico, and has written a True Book about that state.